$\mathcal{T}$his book belongs to

_____

a woman of prayer.

GROWTH & STUDY GUIDE

A Woman's Call to Prayer

Elizabeth George

HARVEST HOUSE PUBLISHERS

EUGENE, OREGON

Cover by Terry Dugan Design, Minneapolis, Minnesota

Cover photo © Victoria Pearson/Botanica/Getty Images

Acknowledgment

As always, thank you to my dear husband, Jim George, M.Div.,Th.M., for your able assistance, guidance, suggestions, and loving encouragement on this project.

A WOMAN'S CALL TO PRAYER GROWTH AND STUDY GUIDE
Copyright © 2004 by Elizabeth George
Published by Harvest House Publishers
Eugene, Oregon 97402
www.harvesthousepublishers.com

ISBN 0-7369-1155-3

Printed in the United States of America

04 05 06 07 08 09 10 11 / BP-CF / 10 9 8 7 6 5 4 3 2 1

Contents

An Invitation to...
Become a Woman of Prayer

Welcome to this helpful and practical hand-book for women like you who desire to make prayer a reality in their busy lives! The book *A Woman's Call to Prayer* and its growth and study guide were written to encourage and motivate you to answer God's call to prayer. This study was created to be:

✓ *Biblical*—You'll use your Bible to interact with the scriptures and answer questions.

✓ *Beneficial*—You'll find yourself growing in your knowledge of the importance of prayer.

✓ *Practical*—You'll discover what you can do —immediately!—to apply what you are learning.

✓ *Inspirational*—You'll want to begin...and continue...your journey into prayer.

A Word of Instruction

This study guide is easy to follow and to do. You'll need your copy of the book *A Woman's Call to Prayer*, your Bible, a pen, and a heart ready to enjoy the blessings of a life of prayer. In each lesson you'll be asked to:

> ≥ Read the corresponding chapter from *A Woman's Call to Prayer.*

> ≥ Answer the questions designed to guide you to a better understanding of prayer and follow through on your desire to become a woman of prayer.

> ≥ Select from the "Checklist for Prayer" in each lesson one way to immediately apply God's Word and fulfill your goal to pray.

> ≥ Write out your personal heart commitments along the way.

A Word for Your Group

Of course, you can grow as you work your way, alone, through the biblical principles presented in this study guide and apply them to your life. But I urge you to share the rich and life-changing journey with other women, with your friends, your neighbors, your Sunday school class or women's Bible study. In a group, no matter how small or large, there is personal care and interest. There is sharing. There are sisters-in-Christ to pray for you. There is the mutual exchange of experiences. There is accountability. And, yes, there is peer pressure…which always helps us to get our lessons done so that glorious growth occurs! And there is sweet, sweet encouragement as you share God's Word with one another and stimulate one another to greater love and good works.

To aid the woman who is guided by God to lead a group, I've included a section in the back of this growth and study guide entitled "Leading a Bible Study Discussion Group." You may also find this information and more on my website, **www.elizabethgeorge.com**.

A Word of Encouragement

No price can be put on a vital prayer life! Through prayer God is honored, your spiritual life is tended, your loved ones are prayed for, and other people and concerns are brought before God's throne of grace. On bended knee, you will find God's grace to help in time of need.

If you will use the insights, tools, and how-to's gained from the book *A Woman's Call to Prayer* and from this growth and study guide, by God's grace and with His help, you can make your desire to pray a reality. You can answer God's call to prayer!

In His everlasting love,

Elizabeth George

$\mathscr{B}$eginning the $\mathscr{J}$ourney into $\mathscr{P}$rayer

In your copy of *A Woman's Call to Prayer,* read the chapter entitled "Beginning the Journey into Prayer." What helped you the most in your desire to become a woman of prayer?

What offered you the greatest challenge?

What information or insights stimulated your desire to be a woman of prayer?

Hearing God's Call to Prayer

I shared my experiences of "hearing" God's call to prayer. Can you remember and share any beginning start-up steps you have taken to launch or accelerate your own journey into prayer?

Making a Commitment

I shared my experience with making a commitment to pray. Have you ever made your own commitment to prayer? If so, share what you did and how it has helped you answer God's call to prayer. If not, what kind of commitment to prayer could you make to begin your own journey into prayer?

*C*hecklist for *P*rayer

✓ *Pray now!*—Have you taken Step 1 yet? If not, let me again urge you to put this study guide down, grab your kitchen timer, and pray for five minutes. Don't go to the next point until you have prayed for those five minutes.

✓ *Get organized*—Round up some kind of notebook. Describe it here, or describe what you are already using and why it works for you. It doesn't have to be elaborate. (Remember my little purple book?)

✓ *Look ahead*—Check out your calendar. What times of the day next week will you schedule for prayer? Begin today, and don't forget to begin using your Prayer Calendar today. (See pages 280-81 in *A Woman's Call to Prayer*.)

Answering God's Call to You

Think about your prayer-life and your new journey into prayer. Then write out in 100 words or less your commitment to make prayer a reality in your life. Ask God to help you carry out these ideas.

Write down God's greatest answer
to your prayers this week.

Don't forget to thank and praise Him!

Ꙩen Reasons Women Don't Pray—Part 1

In your copy of *A Woman's Call to Prayer,* read the chapter entitled "Ten Reasons Women Don't Pray—Part 1." What helped you the most in your desire to become a woman of prayer?

What offered you the greatest challenge?

What information or insights stimulated your desire to be a woman of prayer?

1. *Worldliness* keeps us from praying.

   Read 1 John 2:15-17. What effect does "the world" have on you (verse 16)?

   Read Psalm 107:9. What opposite effect does a passionate hunger and thirst for the things of God have?

   Read Matthew 26:41. What warning and advice does Jesus give?

2. *Busyness* keeps us from praying.

   Read Luke 10:38-42.

   —How did Martha use her time?

   —What effect did Martha's use of her time and energy have on her conduct?

   —How did Mary use her time?

   —What was *the one thing* Mary chose or did that made the difference between the two sisters' behavior?

3. *Foolishness* keeps us from praying.

Read Matthew 6:31-33.

—What is Jesus' command to you in verse 33?

—What is His promise to you in verse 33?

Read 1 John 2:15-17. What happens to the things of this world (verse 17)?

Checklist for Prayer

✓ *Evaluate your heart*—Identify three things you can do to turn your back on the world.

✓ *Evaluate your lifestyle*—Think about your daily routine. How are you spending your time? What one thing could you eliminate to make time for prayer?

✓ *Evaluate your priorities*—Ask God to show you areas of foolishness in your life. Are you wasting your time and life on secondary things?

Answering God's Call to You

Think about your prayer-life as you look at the reasons many women don't pray. Then write out in 100 words or less several new ways to make prayer a reality in your life. Ask God to help you carry out these ideas.

Write down God's greatest answer
to your prayers this week.

Don't forget to thank and praise Him!

Ꮧen Reasons Women Don't Pray—Part 2

 In your copy of *A Woman's Call to Prayer*, read the chapter entitled "Ten Reasons Women Don't Pray—Part 2." What helped you the most in your desire to become a woman of prayer?

What offered you the greatest challenge?

What information or insights stimulated your desire to be a woman of prayer?

To review, write out the first three reasons women don't
pray.

1.

2.

3.

4. *Distance* keeps us from praying.

Read James 4:8. What will help you if you sense any distance between you and God?

Read Hebrews 10:19-22. What additional instruction and
information do you find here for drawing near to God?

Read Psalm 63:8. What did the psalmist say about his
soul (and heart!)?

5. *Ignorance* keeps us from praying.

   What do you learn about God in these scriptures?

   —Ephesians 3:20

   —Philippians 4:19

   —Matthew 7:9-11

   What do you learn about asking God in these scriptures?

   —Jeremiah 33:3

   —James 4:3

   —Matthew 7:7-8

6. *Sinfulness* keeps us from praying.

   How did sin affect these people's relationships with God?

   —Adam and Eve in Genesis 3:8

   —King David in Psalm 32:3

   Read Psalm 139:8-12. Can you hide from God? Please explain.

   What are several solutions the Bible gives for dealing with sin and drawing near to God?

   —Psalm 32:5

   —1 John 1:9

Checklist for Prayer

✓ *Examine your relationship with God*—Are you praying regularly? What does a look at your Prayer Calendar reveal? What is keeping you from prayer, and what must you do?

✓ *Write out verses to memorize*—Begin with the verses below.

—Jeremiah 33:3
—Matthew 7:7-8
—James 4:3

✓ *Search your heart for sin*—Is there "any wicked way" in you? If so, confess it now and thank God for His forgiveness.

Answering God's Call to You

Think about your prayer-life as you look at more reasons women don't pray. Then write out in 100 words or less several new ways for making prayer a reality in your life. Ask God to help you carry out these ideas.

Write down God's greatest answer
to your prayers this week.

Don't forget to thank and praise Him!

Ten Reasons Women Don't Pray—Part 3

In your copy of *A Woman's Call to Prayer*, read the chapter entitled "Ten Reasons Women Don't Pray—Part 3." What helped you the most in your desire to become a woman of prayer?

What offered you the greatest challenge?

What information or insights stimulated your desire to be a woman of prayer?

To review, write out the first six reasons women don't pray.

1.   4.

2.   5.

3.   6.

7. *Faithlessness* keeps us from praying.

   Read James 4:2. What is one reason we don't experience answers to prayer?

   Read Matthew 21:22. This is not a blank check for you to fill in. However, what are the requirements stated here for receiving in prayer?

   Read Matthew 7:7-8. What are Jesus' instructions for prayer?

   How do you think asking in prayer evidences faith?

8. *Pridefulness* keeps us from praying.

   How does the truth of these verses help us guard against pride?

   —2 Chronicles 7:14

   —Psalm 34:18

   —Psalm 51:17

9. *Inexperience* keeps us from praying.

Describe the scene in Luke 11:1.

—Who was present?

—What was happening?

—What question was asked, and by whom?

—How was the question answered (verses 2-4)?

10. *Laziness* keeps us from praying.

Read through Matthew 26:36-46.

—What did Jesus do in verse 39?

—What did He ask of three of the disciples (verse 38)?

—What did the disciples do instead (verse 40)?

—What did Jesus tell them in verse 41?

Write out the two principles from your book that will help with laziness.

—

—

Checklist for Prayer

✓   *Access your faith-quotient*—How would you describe your "faith-quotient"?

✓   *Take time to think*—What keeps you from praying?

✓   *Desire to answer God's call*—How would you describe your desire to answer God's call to prayer?

Think about your prayer-life as you look at more reasons women don't pray. Then write out in 100 words or less several new ways for making prayer a reality in your life. Ask God to help you carry out these ideas.

Write down God's greatest answer
to your prayers this week.

Don't forget to thank and praise Him!

When You Are in Trouble...Pray!

In your copy of *A Woman's Call to Prayer,* read the chapter entitled "When You Are in Trouble...Pray!" What helped you the most in your desire to become a woman of prayer?

What offered you the greatest challenge?

What information or insights stimulated your desire to be a woman of prayer?

In Times of Trouble...Pray!

Queen Esther faced trouble

Read Esther 4:8-17. Note several ways Esther approached her troubles (verses 16 and 17).

King Hezekiah faced trouble

Read through 2 Kings 19:14-19. Note several ways King Hezekiah approached his troubles.

Jesus spoke of trouble

Read Luke 18:1. How do you normally respond to your troubles?

What lessons do Jesus, Esther, and King Hezekiah teach you about your times of trouble?

I have faced trouble

Look up the following verses, and then note which ones you like best, and why.

—Psalm 60:12

—Psalm 37:6

—1 Peter 5:6

—Psalm 143:9

—Psalm 23:5

You will face trouble

Read John 16:33. What is the "bad news" and what is the "good news"?

Read 2 Timothy 3:12. What will happen to you if you seek to live a godly life?

What message do these verses send regarding trouble?

—James 1:2

—1 Peter 4:12

How do these truths alter your perspective on trouble and prepare you to face it?

Checklist for Prayer

✓ *Look at your "Prayer Calendar"*—How is it looking? What is one thing that must change?

✓ *Look for trouble*—Accept trouble as a part of the Christian life. Also remember that wisdom always has a plan. What is your plan for facing trouble, and where does prayer fit in?

✓ *Look for highlights*—Did you name your troubles? How can you put your "plan" to work today?

Answering God's Call to You

Think about prayer and your heart when you are in trouble. Then write out in 100 words or less several new ways for making prayer a reality in your life. Ask God to help you carry out these ideas.

Write down God's greatest answer
to your prayers this week.

Don't forget to thank and praise Him!

When You Are Disappointed by Others...Pray!

In your copy of *A Woman's Call to Prayer*, read the chapter entitled "When You Are Disappointed by Others...Pray!" What helped you the most in your desire to become a woman of prayer?

What offered you the greatest challenge?

What information or insights stimulated your desire to be a woman of prayer?

Pray for Others

Moses prayed for his brother Aaron

Read Exodus 32:19-24 and Deuteronomy 9:18-20. How did Aaron disappoint God and Moses, and what did Moses do?

Moses prayed for God's people

Read Exodus 32:7-11 and 31-32. How did God's people disappoint God and Moses, and what did Moses do?

Job prayed for his friends

Read Job 42:7-10. For 28 chapters in the book of Job, we read how Job's friends charged him with sin as he suffered. What did God require of them, and what did Job do?

A question or two for you

What lessons do these noble pray-ers teach you about praying for those who disappoint you?

When You Are Disappointed by Others...Forgive One Another!

What are some possible dangers of failing to forgive others according to:

—Hebrews 12:15

—Matthew 6:14-15

What better ways does the Bible suggest according to:

—Ephesians 4:32

—Colossians 3:13

—Luke 6:27-28

—1 Corinthians 13:5

When You Are Disappointed by Others...Watch Your Heart!

Samuel prayed

Read 1 Samuel 12:23. What was Samuel's response toward the people who rejected him?

Moses prayed

Read Deuteronomy 9:18-20 and Exodus 32:31-32. What was Moses' response toward his brother and the people who failed God?

Job prayed

Read Job 42:10. What was Job's response toward his friends who wrongly accused him?

When You Are Disappointed by Others...Offer a Helping Hand!

What should your attitude be when others fail?

—Proverbs 24:17-18

—1 Corinthians 10:12

—Galatians 6:1-2

Checklist for Prayer

✓ *Check your prayer-life*—Are you faithfully praying? And are you praying faithfully for those who fail or disappoint you?

✓ *Check your heart*—Is there anyone you are failing to forgive? Then check out Romans 3:23!

✓ *Check your relationships*—Are you following Jesus' instructions in Luke 6:27-28?

Answering God's Call to You

Think about prayer and your heart when you are disappointed by others. Then write out in 100 words or less several new ways for making prayer a reality in your life. Ask God to help you carry out these ideas.

Write down God's greatest answer
to your prayers this week.

Don't forget to thank and praise Him!

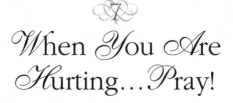

When You Are Hurting...Pray!

In your copy of *A Woman's Call to Prayer,* read the chapter entitled "When You Are Hurting...Pray!" What helped you the most in your desire to become a woman of prayer?

What offered you the greatest challenge?

What information or insights stimulated your desire to be a woman of prayer?

When Your Heart Hurts...Pray!

Meet someone whose heart was hurt

Read Psalm 55:1-15 and briefly describe David's agonizing situation.

Are you someone who's been hurt?

Read these verses and note what they teach regarding suffering.

—John 16:33

—2 Timothy 3:12

—James 1:2

—1 Peter 1:6

Lessons on Praying from a Hurting Heart

Lesson #1—Cast your burden on the Lord

Read Psalm 55:22. What is the message about your burdens?

Read 1 Peter 5:7. Why can you cast your burdens on the Lord, and once you do, what will He do?

Lesson #2—Resist the temptation to run away

Read Psalm 55:6-8 and 16-17. What was David's desire? But what did he do instead?

Read 1 Corinthians 10:13. What is God's promise to you?

Lesson #3—Believe that God will sustain you

Read Psalm 55:16-22. Note a few of the truths about God that David rehearsed and remembered. What was David's final victory cry in verse 23?

Checklist for Prayer

✓ *Stay*—Stand firm. Is there any situation, person, or heartache that is making your life miserable? How does Psalm 55:22 encourage your faith in God?

✓ *Pray*—Look up. Are you praying about your problem? This week make it a point to pray each and every time you think about your painful situation.

✓ *Weigh*— Pay attention. Write out and memorize Romans 8:28-29. This week look for the good that is coming from your trial. Keep a daily "blessings" list, and regularly thank God that you are being transformed into the image of His dear Son.

Answering God's Call to You

Think about prayer and your heart when you are hurting. Then write out in 100 words or less several new ways for making prayer a reality in your life. Ask God to help you carry out these ideas.

Write down God's greatest answer
to your prayers this week.

Don't forget to thank and praise Him!

8

When You Are Worshiping...Pray!

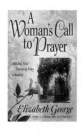

In your copy of *A Woman's Call to Prayer*, read the chapter entitled "When You Are Worshiping...Pray!" What helped you the most in your desire to become a woman of prayer?

What offered you the greatest challenge?

What information or insights stimulated your desire to be a woman of prayer?

The Sweet Aroma of Worship

Worship and Incense

Read Leviticus 1. Note the number of times reference is made to the aroma of the burnt offering.

Read 2 Chronicles 13:11. Describe the "order of worship" in the temple of the Lord.

Read 2 Chronicles 29:28-29. Describe this scene of worship after the temple was restored.

Read Luke 1:8-10. Describe this scene of daily temple worship.

How does this brief look at the Old Testament sacrificial offerings encourage your worship of God through prayer?

The Prayers of True Worshipers

The prayers of a king

Read Psalm 141:2. How does King David refer to his prayers?

The prayers of a priest

Read Luke 1:5-13. Describe Zacharias' honor and duty.

—Describe the people who were present during the offering.

—How did God answer Zacharias' prayers?

The prayers of your heart

Read the following verses and note the instructions given to you concerning your prayer-life.

—Ephesians 6:18

—Colossians 4:2

—1 Thessalonians 5:17

—Hebrews 13:15

Checklist for Prayer

✓   *Sacrifice your carelessness*—List the three suggestions for ordering your prayers. Are all three an established part of your prayer-life? What must you do to answer yes to this question?

✓   *Sacrifice your sin*—Can you think of any favorite sins that must be put away? What is your plan for doing so?

✓   *Sacrifice your heart*—Paul said of those he prayed for, "I have you in my heart" (Philippians 1:7). Who needs your heartfelt prayers?

Answering God's Call to You

Think about prayer and your heart when you are worshiping. Then write out in 100 words or less several new ways for making prayer a reality in your life. Ask God to help you carry out these ideas.

Write down God's greatest answer
to your prayers this week.

Don't forget to thank and praise Him!

9

When You Are Worried...Pray!

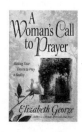 In your copy of *A Woman's Call to Prayer,* read the chapter entitled "When You Are Worried...Pray!" What helped you the most in your desire to become a woman of prayer?

What offered you the greatest challenge?

What information or insights stimulated your desire to be a woman of prayer?

God Commands, "Do Not Worry!"

The command— "Be anxious for nothing"

Read Philippians 1:27-28. What problems did these people face?

Read Philippians 3:1-2. What is another problem the Philippians had to deal with?

Read 2 Corinthians 12:7. What difficulty did Paul have to cope with daily?

The scope of the command— "Be anxious for nothing"

What problems and difficulties do you tend to worry about?

What message does God's command send to your heart?

The solution—Prayer

By prayer—Read 1 Peter 5:7. Pay careful attention to each word. What is its advice for your worries?

By supplication—Read Hebrews 4:16. How does prayer help with the issues of your life?

With thanksgiving—Read Romans 8:28-29. Make a brief list of items for thanksgiving...even in the midst of your trials.

By requests—Have you created a list of prayer "requests" in your prayer notebook? How do you think praying faithfully for your requests counteracts worrying?

The result—"The peace of God"

Read Philippians 4:7. Describe the peace of God and its effects on your heart.

Checklist for Prayer

✓ *Don't...*miss a day of prayer—How does daily prayer give you God's peace for your daily concerns?

✓ *Do...*memorize Psalm 23—Write the familiar psalm on cards and carry them with you. You cannot worry and think about God's power, presence, and care at the same time! Do you agree? Why or why not?

✓ *Do...*determine a "worry day"—It's a mental discipline...and it works! What day will you choose for revisiting your "worries"? (Be sure to keep a record of what "happens" to all your worries in one week's time.)

Think about prayer and your heart when you are worried. Then write out in 100 words or less several new ways for making prayer a reality in your life. Ask God to help you carry out these ideas.

Write down God's greatest answer
to your prayers this week.

Don't forget to thank and praise Him!

10
When You Are Overwhelmed...Pray!

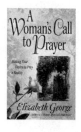

In your copy of *A Woman's Call to Prayer,* read the chapter entitled "When You Are Overwhelmed...Pray!" What helped you the most in your desire to become a woman of prayer?

What offered you the greatest challenge?

What information or insights stimulated your desire to be a woman of prayer?

Trust in God's Help with Prayer

Read Romans 8:26-27. How does the Holy Spirit help you pray, according to...

—verse 26?

—verse 27?

How does this ministry of the Holy Spirit give you confidence when...

—you don't know how to pray?

—you don't know the will of God?

A Personal Word of Testimony

A red-letter day

I shared one of my seemingly overwhelming experiences. Can you recall one of yours? Note it here.

Overwhelmed by emotions

Read Psalm 18:4-6 and Psalm 61:2. Describe the emotions of the psalmist. Also describe his solution.

God's grace to me

   Read 2 Corinthians 12:9. How is God's grace described?

   Read Romans 8:26-27. What special ministry does the Holy Spirit have to believers?

The end of the story

   Read Romans 8:28-29. What is one aspect of "the end of the story" we can count on as believers?

A word for you

   Read Ephesians 5:20 and 1 Thessalonians 5:18. What words of encouragement and instruction do they contain?

Checklist for Prayer

✓   *Do your best*—Even when you are overwhelmed, what
     is God's comfort found in Philippians 4:7?

✓   *Try to pray*—Most people agree the first step toward any
     worthwhile thing is always the hardest. What will your
     first step into prayer during difficult times be?

✓   *Watch your heart*—What advice and guidelines does
     Psalm 19:14 have for your prayer-life and your heart?

Answering God's Call to You

Think about prayer and your heart when you are over-whelmed. Then write out in 100 words or less several new ways for making prayer a reality in your life. Ask God to help you carry out these ideas.

Write down God's greatest answer
to your prayers this week.

Don't forget to thank and praise Him!

When You Are in Need...Pray!

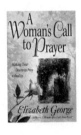

In your copy of *A Woman's Call to Prayer*, read the chapter entitled "When You Are in Need...Pray!" What helped you the most in your desire to become a woman of prayer?

What offered you the greatest challenge?

What information or insights stimulated your desire to be a woman of prayer?

Make Your Needs Known to God

Review the list of some of the men and women of the Bible. What strikes you about their needs?

What strikes you about their response?

Praying About Your Personal Needs

Health and energy—Where, when, and for what could you use better health and greater energy? Is this need on your prayer list, and are you praying about it?

Attitude—Look at Galatians 5:22-23. What attitudes listed there are lacking in your life or need improvement? Are there needs on your prayer list, and are you praying about them?

Faithfulness—Look at 1 Timothy 3:11. Where do you need to be more faithful? Is this need on your prayer list, and are you praying about it?

Finances—What are your needs in the Financial Department? Is this need on your prayer list, and are you praying about it?

Work—Look at Proverbs 31:13 and Colossians 3:23. Is this need on your prayer list, and are you praying about it?

Wisdom—Look at James 1:5. What wisdom do you need today? Daily? Is this need on your prayer list, and are you praying about it?

Relationships—Think through your relationships and list the five that are the most important to you. Do any of these relationships have special "needs"? Are the needs on your prayer list, and are you praying about them?

Praying About Your Needs as a Married Woman

Read these verses and note how you need to pray regarding each in your marriage situation:

—Genesis 2:18

—Ephesians 5:22-24 and Colossians 3:18

—Ephesians 5:33

—Titus 2:4

Praying About Your Personal Needs as a Mother

Read these verses and note how you need to pray regarding each in your parenting situation:

—Proverbs 31:15

—Proverbs 31:27

—Ephesians 6:4

—Titus 2:4

Checklist for Prayer

✓ *Pray daily*—Just as God's people needed daily manna, or food from heaven (Exodus 16:4), you need God's strength and wisdom each day. Are you praying for your needs? Are you praying daily? What changes need to be made?

✓ *Tithe your time*—What portion or percentage of your time each day would you say you are giving to God? What changes need to be made to ensure you have a "time" for expressing your needs to God each day?

✓ *Memorize Scripture*—Follow the instructions for writing out and memorizing Philippians 4:6. What are the instructions of the verse regarding your needs?

Answering God's Call to You

Think about prayer and your heart when you are in need. Then write out in 100 words or less several new ways for making prayer a reality in your life. Ask God to help you carry out these ideas.

Write down God's greatest answer
to your prayers this week.

Don't forget to thank and praise Him!

12

When You Must Make a Decision...Pray for Faith!

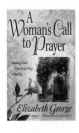 In your copy of *A Woman's Call to Prayer,* read the chapter entitled "When You Must Make a Decision...Pray for Faith!" What helped you the most in your desire to become a woman of prayer?

What offered you the greatest challenge?

What information or insights stimulated your desire to be a woman of prayer?

No Decision Made Without Prayer!

King Solomon prayed

Read 1 Kings 3:6-12. What impresses you most about Solomon's prayer?

Nehemiah prayed

Read Nehemiah 1:4-11. What impresses you most about Nehemiah's prayer?

Queen Esther prayed

Read Esther 4:16. What impresses you most about Esther's prayer and spiritual preparations?

The apostle Paul prayed

Read Acts 9:6-9. What impresses you most about Paul's prayer and spiritual preparations?

King David prayed

Read Psalm 5:3; 55:17; and 63:1. What impresses you most about David's prayer-life?

The Lord Jesus prayed

Read Mark 1:35-39. What appears to have happened during Jesus' time of prayer?

You Are Called to a Life of Faith

1. *You are called to act in confidence.*

    Read Romans 14:5 and 23, and 1 John 3:21. What difference should prayer and careful thought make in your choices and your confidence?

2. *You are called to pray for confidence.*

    Read Acts 4:23-31. After praying, how did the early Christians act in faith and confidence?

3. *You are called to enjoy peace of mind.*

    How will a clear conscience and a fully persuaded mind (Romans 14:5) lead to peace of mind as you move forward after praying and making a decision?

Checklist for Prayer

✓   *Commit to pray*—List some benefits to a *No decision made without prayer* commitment. Have you made your commitment yet?

✓   *Set up to pray*—If you haven't already, create a "Decisions to Make" page. Begin writing *every* decision to be made there. When will you begin?

✓   *Ask as you pray*—Note the seven questions listed in your book that will help guide you to decisions that better reflect God's will and strengthen your faith in His leading. Look at each scripture and note its message here: Then slip this exercise into the "Decisions to Be Made" section in your prayer notebook.

> Excess—
>
> Expediency—
>
> Emulation—
>
> Evangelism—
>
> Edification—
>
> Exaltation—
>
> Example—

Answering God's Call to You

Think about the role of faith in making decisions and finding God's will. Then write out in 100 words or less several new ways for making prayer a reality in your life. Ask God to help you carry out these ideas.

Write down God's greatest answer
to your prayers this week.

Don't forget to thank and praise Him!

13

When You Must Make a Decision...Pray for Wisdom!—Part 1

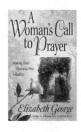 In your copy of *A Woman's Call to Prayer,* read the chapter entitled "When You Must Make a Decision...Pray for Wisdom!—Part 1." What helped you the most in your desire to become a woman of prayer?

What offered you the greatest challenge?

What information or insights stimulated your desire to be a woman of prayer?

You Are Called to a Life of Wisdom

No decision made without prayer.

Have you made this a rule in your decision-making yet? Can you share an instance or two where God guided you or gave you wisdom?

If not, read James 1:5. What instructions are given for obtaining wisdom, and what is God's promise?

The Workings of Wisdom

Wisdom fears the Lord

Read Proverbs 9:10. What are the instructions for gaining wisdom and understanding?

Wisdom applies God's Word to everyday life

Read Matthew 6:33-34. How important is today, and how should today be lived?

Wisdom sees life from God's perspective

Read Proverbs 1:10-19. How does this passage in the Bible teach God's perspective to someone who could make foolish choices?

Wisdom follows the best course of action

Read Proverbs 1:20-23. To whom is wisdom available? What is the hearer's responsibility?

Putting God's Wisdom to Work in Your Life

First...pray to God for help.

Read James 1:5. What do you need God's wisdom for today? How do you think asking God for wisdom will help you discern God's will?

Second...pray through James 4:17.

Read James 4:17. Is the desire of your heart to do right, to do good, to do the right thing? How do you think asking God to show you the right thing to do will help you walk in His will?

Finally...pray through Proverbs 3:5-6.

Read Proverbs 3:5-6. How do you think acknowledging God in all your ways will lead you to God's appointed will?

Checklist for Prayer

✓ *Pinpoint...*your Number One problem area—Then begin using James 1:5, 4:17, and Proverbs 3:5-6 to guide you to greater wisdom.

✓ *Purpose...*to pray daily—Again, use the above verses to guide you as you seek to make decisions that reflect God's will and wisdom.

✓ *Pray...*faithfully—Don't forget to record your decisions and progress in your prayer notebook and to mark your Prayer Calendar.

Think about the role of wisdom in making decisions and finding God's will. Then write out in 100 words or less several new ways for making prayer a reality in your life. Ask God to help you carry out these ideas.

Write down God's greatest answer
to your prayers this week.

Don't forget to thank and praise Him!

14

*W*hen *Y*ou *M*ust *M*ake a *D*ecision…*P*ray for *W*isdom!—Part 2

 In your copy of *A Woman's Call to Prayer*, read the chapter entitled "When You Must Make a Decision…Pray for Wisdom!—Part 2." What helped you the most in your desire to become a woman of prayer?

What offered you the greatest challenge?

What information or insights stimulated your desire to be a woman of prayer?

Remember What You Know

1. *Your relationship with God*

   Read Luke 22:42 and Acts 9:6. How did Jesus' and Paul's relationship with God affect their prayers and actions? How should your relationship with God affect you and your prayers? Does it? Please explain.

2. *Your walk with God*

   Read Psalm 19:14; Galatians 5:16; 5:22-23; and Ephesians 4:1. List new ways you should apply these standards to your daily walk.

3. *Your desire to find God's will*

   Read Psalm 139:23-24; 5:3; and James 5:16. How can you intensify your prayers to know God's will?

4. *Your weapons for the battle*

   Read James 1:5; 4:17; and Proverbs 3:5-6. How do you think these "weapons" would help you discern God's will for your day and your life?

Putting God's Wisdom to Work in Your Life

How do you think prayer could affect the following areas of your life?

Your relationships—

Your finances—

Your time—

Your job—

Your parents—

Circle the areas where you need to be more faithful in prayer.

*C*hecklist for *P*rayer

✓ *Create a list*—What personal issues and relationships need your attention in prayer?

✓ *Ask for help*—Place your list in your prayer notebook and begin to pray fervently and faithfully. What is the promise of James 5:16?

✓ *Affirm your desire*—Based on Acts 13:22, what reveals a woman after God's own heart? Revisit your commitment to seek God's will and wisdom.

Think again about the role of wisdom in making decisions and finding God's will. Then write out in 100 words or less several more new ways for making prayer a reality in your life. Ask God to help you carry out these ideas.

Write down God's greatest answer
to your prayers this week.

Don't forget to thank and praise Him!

15

When You Must Make a Decision...Pray for Order!

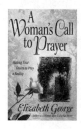

In your copy of *A Woman's Call to Prayer,* read the chapter entitled "When You Must Make a Decision...Pray for Order!" What helped you the most in your desire to become a woman of prayer?

What offered you the greatest challenge?

What information or insights stimulated your desire to be a woman of prayer?

Oh, What a Difference Prayer Makes!

Can you describe a day when your life lacked order because you didn't pray?

Oh, What a Difference Order Makes!

1. *Priorities*—Make a list of your priorities based on how you spend your time. Do they match up with those listed from God's Word in your book? What changes need to be made?

2. *Planning*—Look at the list of the benefits of planning in your book. Which are true of your life...and which need improving? What changes need to be made?

3. *Scheduling*—What grade would you give yourself in the area of attention to planning? (Circle one.)

A   B   C   D   F

What changes need to be made?

Checklist for Prayer

✓ *Pray over every activity*—Keep records or notes of the process and the scriptures you use to determine God's will. Again, what tale is your Prayer Calendar telling regarding your time spent in prayer and seeking God's will?

✓ *Say no often*—Is it hard or easy for you to say no? Why or why not?

✓ *Make graciousness a goal*—Do you yearn for a more gracious lifestyle, as opposed to the helter-skelter breathlessness that surrounds most busy women? How will prayer help?

Answering God's Call to You

Think about the role of order in making decisions and finding God's will. Then write out in 100 words or less several new ways for making prayer a reality in your life. Ask God to help you carry out these ideas.

Write down God's greatest answer
to your prayers this week.

Don't forget to thank and praise Him!

16

When You Must Make a Decision...Pray for Understanding!

In your copy of *A Woman's Call to Prayer,* read the chapter entitled "When You Must Make a Decision...Pray for Understanding!" What helped you the most in your desire to become a woman of prayer?

What offered you the greatest challenge?

What information or insights stimulated your desire to be a woman of prayer?

Discovering God's Will

Read Proverbs 3:5-6, paying attention to each word. What is God's promise regarding His will in verse 6?

What is your part in discovering God's will according to:
—verse 5

—verse 5

—verse 6

Four Questions for Your Heart

To begin this exercise, write down one decision you are trying to make. Create a prayer page and begin praying through the four questions.

Question 1: Why would I do this?

(Remember to confess any unbiblical motives.)

Question 2: Why would I not do this?

(Remember to rule out anything that goes against God's Word.)

Question 3: Why should I do this?

(Remember to look for reasons from God's Word.)

Question 4: Why should I not do this?

(Remember your goal is to obey and please God.)

Checklist for Prayer

✓   *Do it now!* Stop making decisions that you don't pray about! How are you doing on *No decisions made without prayer?* Have you learned to wait until you've prayed? Share where you are in this vital prayer process.

✓   *Do it now!* Create a "Decisions to Make" section in your prayer notebook. Is your prayer notebook being put to good use? Share how it has aided your prayer-life and your decision-making.

✓   *Do it now!* Make a list of the decisions you need to make, one page for each. How good are you at saying no while you are in the process of praying to know God's will?

Answering God's Call to You

Think about the role of understanding in making decisions and finding God's will. Then write out in 100 words or less several new ways for making prayer a reality in your life. Ask God to help you carry out these ideas.

Write down God's greatest answer
to your prayers this week.

Don't forget to thank and praise Him!

𝒯he 𝒯ime of 𝒫rayer

 In your copy of *A Woman's Call to Prayer,* read the chapter entitled "The Time of Prayer." What helped you the most in your desire to become a woman of prayer?

What offered you the greatest challenge?

What information or insights stimulated your desire to be a woman of prayer?

Learning About Prayer

Read Luke 11:1—Describe the scene here.

—Who was present?

—What was Jesus doing?

—What did one of Jesus' disciples ask of Him?

Read Luke 11:2-4.

—How did Jesus answer the disciples?

—What impresses you about Jesus' answer?

How does this narrative encourage and instruct you in learning more about prayer?

Choosing a Time for Personal Prayer

Note a few of the "times" when God's people prayed. What message do they send to your heart?

As you think about your lifestyle, schedule, and demands, what time do you think is best for you to be consistent and faithful in praying daily?

Checklist for Prayer

✓ *First, get organized*—Did you set a time for prayer? Is it on your daily schedule? Have you scheduled your prayer time for at least the next week? If not, do so now. Why did you choose this time?

✓ *Second, get ready*—List here the tools and environment that will help to make your decision to pray a reality. Round up these items...and get to bed early!

✓ *Third, get up*—As the saying goes, the secret to getting up is "mind over mattress." What can you do to make your plan to get up and pray happen? List at least three things you can do to ensure you have a "time" of prayer.

Answering God's Call to You

Think about time as a part of God's formula for effective prayer. Then write out in 100 words or less several new ways for making prayer a reality in your life. Ask God to help you carry out these ideas.

Write down God's greatest answer
to your prayers this week.

Don't forget to thank and praise Him!

18
The Times of Prayer

In your copy of *A Woman's Call to Prayer*, read the chapter entitled "The Times of Prayer." What helped you the most in your desire to become a woman of prayer?

What offered you the greatest challenge?

What information or insights stimulated your desire to be a woman of prayer?

"Call to Me"

Read Jeremiah 33:3. What does God ask of us? What does He promise?

Times of emergency—Recount a few of your own 9-1-1 calls to God. What happened, and how did God answer?

Times of fighting for the family—Read John 11:1-3. Who made a 9-1-1 call to Jesus and why? Think of a family member who needs you to battle for him or her in prayer. Is someone in your family an unbeliever? A prodigal? Away from home? Having to make a hard decision? Physically fighting for their life?

Times of wrestling for the ministry—Read Ephesians 6:18-20 and Colossians 4:2-4. What are some of the prayer requests Paul shared regarding his ministry? What ministry endeavors can you add to your prayer list?

Times of distress and disaster—Read Mark 14:32-36. What was Jesus' distressing situation here? How did He handle it? What did He ask of Peter, James, and John? Who do you know who is currently in a time of distress, and how can you pray faithfully for him or her?

Checklist for Prayer

✓ *Consider fasting*—Have you ever fasted? If so, share a little about your experience. If not, pray about this spiritual discipline, and talk to others about it.

✓ *Continue praying*—Don't stop praying! Don't lose heart! Is there someone you need to begin praying for again? What is his or her situation? Give that person a check-up call, list him or her again in your prayer notebook...and pray!

✓ *Count your blessings*—Make a page in your prayer notebook for recording God's benefits and blessings. God asks us not to forget His blessings (Psalm 103:2). Be sure you bless others by sharing with them about how God has blessed you.

Answering God's Call to You

Think about times of prayer as a part of God's formula for effective prayer. Then write out in 100 words or less several new ways for making prayer a reality in your life. Ask God to help you carry out these ideas.

Write down God's greatest answer
to your prayers this week.

Don't forget to thank and praise Him!

19

ℭℎe 𝒫lace of 𝒫rayer

In your copy of *A Woman's Call to Prayer*, read the chapter entitled "The Place of Prayer." What helped you the most in your desire to become a woman of prayer?

What offered you the greatest challenge?

What information or insights stimulated your desire to be a woman of prayer?

Is There a Proper Place to Pray?

Read John 4:19-24. What is the most important element of true worship, of which prayer is a part?

Read these scriptures for yourself and note the variety of places where prayer occurred:

—Acts 1:12-14

—Acts 10:9

—Acts 16:13

—Acts 16:25

—Acts 21:5

My Journey to a Place of Prayer

What pages, such as "spititual growth list," can you add to your prayer notebook that will help you remember to pray?

The Places of Prayer for Others

Did you learn anything new, or receive any good ideas regarding places of prayer?

What messages do these pray-ers send your way regarding prayer?

The Place of Prayer for You

Read Matthew 6:5-6.

—What are Jesus' instructions regarding a place of prayer?

—What is Jesus' message regarding your motives in your prayer times?

—What does Jesus teach regarding your heavenly Father?

Checklist for Prayer

✓   *Describe*...your place of prayer.

✓   *Decide*...where your place will be if you don't yet have one.

✓   *Provide*...what is missing or what would improve your prayer place. Make your list of items here.

Think about place as a part of God's formula for effective prayer. Then write out in 100 words or less several new ways for making prayer a reality in your life. Ask God to help you carry out these ideas.

Write down God's greatest answer
to your prayers this week.

Don't forget to thank and praise Him!

❧ 20

ℭhe Posture of Prayer

In your copy of *A Woman's Call to Prayer,* read the chapter entitled "The Posture of Prayer." What helped you the most in your desire to become a woman of prayer?

What offered you the greatest challenge?

What information or insights stimulated your desire to be a woman of prayer?

How Then Should We Pray?

Read the following scriptures and note the variety of postures mentioned:

—Exodus 4:31

—Numbers 16:22

—1 Samuel 1:26

—2 Samuel 12:16

—1 Kings 8:54

—1 Kings 18:42 and James 5:18

—Jonah 2:1

—Ezra 10:1

—Luke 18:13

—Matthew 26:39

What is the key message to your heart from these faithful
pray-ers?

"When You Pray..."

Read Matthew 6:5-6.

What do you learn about the two types of prayers and prayers Jesus referred to?

What is revealed about their hearts?

What is Jesus' message to your heart?

Checklist for Prayer

✓ *Be sure*—Are your motives for the posture of your prayers pure? Are you seeking to draw attention to yourself and your spirituality?

✓ *Be sure*—Are you spending the majority of your time in prayer out of the public eye? Look at Matthew 6:5-6. What did Jesus lay down as His guidelines for prayer?

✓ *Be sure*—Are you a lady in all that you do? Could your prayer posture be a distraction to others as they seek to pray and worship?

Answering God's Call to You

Think about posture as a part of God's formula for effective prayer. Then write out in 100 words or less several new ways for making prayer a reality in your life. Ask God to help you carry out these ideas.

Write down God's greatest answer
to your prayers this week.

Don't forget to thank and praise Him!

The Voice of Prayer

 In your copy of *A Woman's Call to Prayer,* read the chapter entitled "The Voice of Prayer." What helped you the most in your desire to become a woman of prayer?

What offered you the greatest challenge?

What information or insights stimulated your desire to be a woman of prayer?

God's Voices of Prayer

What do you learn about the voice of prayer from these faithful pray-ers in the Bible?

—1 Samuel 1:10-13

—Ezra 10:1

—Psalm 5:3

—Psalm 63:6

—Psalm 26:7

—Psalm 119:64

—Matthew 14:30

Your Heart Is Your Voice

Read the following verses and note what they teach about sin and God's response to the one praying:

—Psalm 66:18

—Job 27:8-9

—Proverbs 1:23-28

—Proverbs 28:9

Read 1 John 3:21-22 and share the contrast.

Read Psalm 139:23-24. What was David's prayer?

Checklist for Prayer

✓ *Pray regularly*—You will never have a voice of prayer if you don't pray. How does your Prayer Calendar look? Is there anything you must do to pray more regularly?

✓ *Pray penitently*—Examine your heart. Make it a daily habit to search your heart and life for sin. Then confess it once again and lift your voice of prayer.

✓ *Pray Scripture*—Look at these "hands-off verses," and then put them to use when you pray.

—Psalm 46:10

—Psalm 56:4

—Psalm 108:13

—Psalm 138:8

Answering God's Call to You

Think about voice as a part of God's formula for effective prayer. Then write out in 100 words or less several new ways for making prayer a reality in your life. Ask God to help you carry out these ideas.

Write down God's greatest answer
to your prayers this week.

Don't forget to thank and praise Him!

22

Ten Ways to Improve Your Prayer-Life—Part 1

 In your copy of *A Woman's Call to Prayer,* read the chapter entitled "Ten Ways to Improve Your Prayer-Life—Part 1." What helped you the most in your desire to become a woman of prayer?

What offered you the greatest challenge?

What information or insights stimulated your desire to be a woman of prayer?

1. *Use a prayer list or notebook.*

God remembers all your needs, concerns, and situations, but a prayer list or notebook helps you remember them. Have you created your list or notebook? If so, share how you have been blessed. How have you seen God work as you have sought to answer His call to prayer?

2. *Schedule a prayer time each day.*

Have you chosen a time for prayer? Share how you selected this time, and any struggles you have encountered. If you have yet to choose a time, don't wait. God has a great blessing in store once you decide on a time to meet with Him.

3. *Spend time praying with others.*

Have you joined with someone or with a group for prayer? You can be blessed as you hear the hearts of others in a group. If your church has a scheduled corporate prayer time, pay it a visit, and enter into this meaningful time of prayer.

4. *Pray using Scripture.*

Select several favorite prayer passages or verses from the Bible. Start off your prayer time with one of them. This will do wonders in getting you into the flow of prayer. God loves to hear His own words so recite back to God His wonderful Word! What will one prayer passage be?

5. *Borrow from the prayers of others.*

When we pray the prayers of others, we are standing on their shoulders as we use what they have written, and in most cases, prayed to God. Many powerful prayers have been read—and prayed—through the centuries. Get a few books that contain the prayers of others. Take advantage of the wisdom and passion great men and women of God have shared in their vibrant prayers. What could your first step be?

*C*hecklist for *P*rayer

✓ *Pray with others*—Have you found someone who enjoys a vital prayer-life? And have you taken the next step and scheduled a time to pray with her? If not, what will you do this week?

✓ *Pray using Scripture*—List three scriptures you plan to use to get you started on "praying Scripture." If you draw a blank, start with Colossians 1:9-14.

—

—

—

✓ *Pray the prayers of others*—Have you picked up or borrowed a copy of any of the "Suggested Books of Prayer"? (See page 274 in your book.) Have you asked others for the titles of their favorite books? Does your church library have any of these? You are in for a blessing!

Answering God's Call to You

Think about the first five ways to improve your prayer-life. Then write out in 100 words or less several new ways for making prayer a reality in your life. Ask God to help you carry out these ideas.

Write down God's greatest answer
to your prayers this week.

Don't forget to thank and praise Him!

23

Ten Ways to Improve Your Prayer-Life—Part 2

In your copy of *A Woman's Call to Prayer,* read the chapter entitled "Ten Ways to Improve Your Prayer-Life—Part 2." What helped you the most in your desire to become a woman of prayer?

What offered you the greatest challenge?

What information or insights stimulated your desire to be a woman of prayer?

Continuing on from our last chapter, let's add five more "ways" to improve your prayer-life.

6. *Open and close each day with a time of prayer.*

   Have you begun the practice of starting and ending your day with prayer? If so, share how prayer has been the "key of the morning" and the "bolt of the night." If not, how can the quote in your book inspire you to open and close your day with prayer?

7. *Gain inspiration from the biographies of others who prayed.*

   Have you started reading the biographies of famous pray-ers? If so, write down the names of those you have been reading about, and share a quote or story from their lives that has inspired you. If not, take a trip to your church library or visit your local Christian or on-line bookstore. You can also ask people who are pray-ers for the names of others who have inspired them to pray. Then find out about their lives.

8. *Reflect on and study the prayers of the Bible.*

Read Luke 1:46-55. Take time now and answer these questions about Mary's prayer of praise.

—What did Mary say about how God was working in her life, and what was her attitude (verses 46-48)?

—What did Mary say about God and His work (verses 49-50)?

—What did Mary say about God sending His Son (verses 51-53)?

—What did Mary say about God fulfilling His promise to Israel (verses 54-55)?

Now try your hand at 1 Samuel 2:1-10, noting the content of Hannah's prayer.

9. *Follow through with your resolve: No decision made without prayer.*

   Share one instance where you followed through and prayed before making a decision. What was the result?

10. *Feed your heart and mind with God's Word.*

   This is obviously the greatest way to improve your prayer-life. You can't help but have something to say to God if His Word is oozing out of every pore of your body. Each action you take will have God's blessing written all over it, because His Word came to your mind, heart, and lips as you made your decision. Feeding your heart and mind with God's Word will also enable you to freely and effortlessly utter it back to Him in prayer.

   What are your favorite scriptures that inspire you to pray?

Checklist for Prayer

✓ *Learn*...to leave things undone—What culprits, habits, or pet irritations keep you from praying? How can you turn your back on them?

✓ *Learn*...to switch disciplines—Make a brief list of the disciplines you have already mastered. Which one can you postpone each day to fit the discipline of prayer into your day and your life?

✓ *Learn*...to combine disciplines—What other disciplines can you combine with prayer? How and when will you begin?

Answering God's Call to You

Think about the second five ways to improve your prayer-life. Then write out in 100 words or less several new ways for making prayer a reality in your life. Ask God to help you carry out these ideas.

Write down God's greatest answer
to your prayers this week.

Don't forget to thank and praise Him!

24

When You Are Anywhere and at Any Time...Pray!

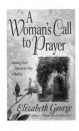 In your copy of *A Woman's Call to Prayer*, read the chapter entitled "When You Are Anywhere and at Any Time...Pray!" What helped you the most in your desire to become a woman of prayer?

What offered you the greatest challenge?

What information or insights stimulated your desire to be a woman of prayer?

You Can Pray Anywhere!

Read Nehemiah 2:1-10.

—What was Nehemiah doing (verse 1)?

—What question did his employer ask (verses 2-4)?

—What did Nehemiah do right away (verse 4)?

—What were the results (verses 5-10)?

Read Jonah 1:7—2:10.

—Where was Jonah? What did he do (Jonah 2:1-9)?

—What were the results (Jonah 2:10)?

You Can Pray at Any Time!

Read again the example of the servant named Mary and her practice of prayer. Which of her prayer habits do you already practice?

Which of her prayer habits could you put into practice? (Also please note: She was praying Scripture!)

You Can Pray All the Time!

Read Ephesians 6:18. What commands are given regarding prayer?

—

—

How does the Holy Spirit help us according to the following scriptures?

—Romans 8:26

—Romans 8:27

—Ephesians 2:18

—Romans 8:15-16

—Galatians 4:6

How can you begin to order your life more around God and His desires, so that you can begin to make prayer your habitual response to every situation throughout your days?

Checklist for Prayer

✓ *Pray*—The Bible tells you to pray. Reflect on what ingredients in God's formula you desire to put into practice. What are they, and what is your plan to do so?

✓ *Praise*—You can also be praising God anywhere, any time, for any circumstance. What is your plan for making this a habit?

✓ *Proceed*—Now look at the Table of Contents. Since you began reading this book, how has your prayer-life changed or improved?

Answering God's Call to You

As we come to this final chapter, think about praying anywhere and at any time. Then write out in 100 words or less several new ways for making prayer a reality in your life. Ask God to help you carry out these ideas.

Write down God's greatest answer
to your prayers this week.

Don't forget to thank and praise Him!

Leading a Bible Study Discussion Group

*W*hat a privilege it is to lead a Bible study! And what joy and excitement await you as you delve into the Word of God and help others to discover its life-changing truths. If God has called you to lead a Bible study group, I know you'll be spending much time in prayer and planning and giving much thought to being an effective leader. I also know that taking the time to read through the following tips will help you to navigate the challenges of leading a Bible study discussion group and enjoying the effort and opportunity.

The Leader's Roles

As a Bible study group leader, you'll find your role changing back and forth from *leader* to *cheerleader* to *lover* to *referee* during the course of a session.

Since you're the leader, group members will look to you to be the *leader* guiding them through the material. So be well prepared. In fact, be over-prepared so that you know the material better than any group member does. Start your study early in the week and let its message simmer all week long. (You might even work several lessons ahead so that you have in mind the big picture and the overall direction of the study.) Be ready to share some additional gems that your group members wouldn't have discovered on their own. That extra insight from your study time—or that comment from a wise Bible teacher or scholar, that clever saying, that keen observation from another believer, and even an appropriate joke—adds an element of fun and keeps Bible study from becoming routine, monotonous, and dry.

Next, be ready to be the group's *cheerleader.* Your energy and enthusiasm for the task at hand can be contagious. It can also stimulate people to get more involved in their personal study as well as in the group discussion.

Third, be the *lover,* the one who shows a genuine concern for the members of the group. You're the one who will establish the atmosphere of the group. If you laugh and have fun, the group members will laugh and have fun. If you hug, they will hug. If you care, they will care. If you share, they will share. If you love, they will love. So pray every day to love the women God has placed in your group. Ask Him to show you how to love them with His love.

Finally, as the leader, you'll need to be the *referee* on occasion. That means making sure everyone has an equal opportunity to speak. That's easier to do when you operate under the assumption that every member of the group has something worthwhile to contribute. So, trusting that the Lord has taught each person during the week, act on that assumption.

Leader, cheerleader, lover, and referee—these four roles of the leader may make the task seem overwhelming. But that's not bad if it keeps you on your knees praying for your group.

A Good Start

Beginning on time, greeting people warmly, and opening in prayer gets the study off to a good start. Know what you want to have happen during your time together and make sure those things get done. That kind of order means comfort for those involved.

Establish a format and let the group members know what that format is. People appreciate being in a Bible study that focuses on the Bible. So keep the discussion on the topic and move the group through the questions. Tangents are often hard to avoid—and even harder to rein in. So be sure to focus on the answers to questions about the specific passage at hand. After all, the purpose of the group is Bible study!

Finally, as someone has accurately observed, "Personal growth is one of the by-products of any effective small group. This growth is achieved when people are recognized and accepted by others. The more friendliness, mutual trust, respect, and warmth exhibited, the more likely that the member will find pleasure in the group, and, too, the more likely she will work hard toward the accomplishment of the group's goals. The effective leader will strive to reinforce desirable traits" (source unknown).

A Dozen Helpful Tips

Here is a list of helpful suggestions for leading a Bible study discussion group:

1. Arrive early, ready to focus fully on others and give of yourself. If you have to do any last-minute preparation, review, re-grouping, or praying, do it in the car. Don't dash in, breathless, harried, late, still tweaking your plans.

2. Check out your meeting place in advance. Do you have everything you need—tables, enough chairs, a blackboard, hymnals if you plan to sing, coffee, etc.?

3. Greet each person warmly by name as she arrives. After all, you've been praying for these women all week long, so let each VIP know that you're glad she's arrived.

4. Use name tags for at least the first two or three weeks.

5. Start on time no matter what—even if only one person is there!

6. Develop a pleasant but firm opening statement. You might say, "This lesson was great! Let's get started so we can enjoy all of it!" or "Let's pray before we begin our lesson."

7. Read the questions, but don't hesitate to reword them on occasion. Rather than reading an entire paragraph of instructions, for instance, you might say, "Question 1 asks us to list some ways that Christ displayed humility. Lisa, please share one way Christ displayed humility."

8. Summarize or paraphrase the answers given. Doing so will keep the discussion focused on the topic, eliminate digressions, help avoid or clear up any misunderstandings of the text, and keep each group member aware of what the others are saying.

9. Keep moving and don't add any of your own questions to the discussion time. It's important to get through the study guide questions. So if a cut-and-dried answer is called for, you don't need to comment with anything other than a "thank you." But when the question asks for an opinion or an application (for instance, "How can this truth help us in our marriages?" or "How do *you* find time for your quiet time?"), let all who want to contribute do so.

10. Affirm each person who contributes, especially if the contribution was very personal, painful to share, or a quiet person's rare statement. Acknowledge everyone who shares a hero by saying something like "Thank you for sharing that insight from your own life" or "We certainly appreciate what God has taught you. Thank you for letting us in on it."

11. Watch your watch, put a clock right in front of you, or consider using a timer. Pace the discussion so that you meet your cut-off time, especially if you want time to pray. Stop at the designated time even if you haven't finished the lesson. Remember that everyone has worked through the study once; you are simply going over it again.

12. End on time. You can only make friends with your group members by ending on time or even a little early! Besides, members of your group have the next item on their agenda to attend to—picking up children from the nursery, babysitter, or school; heading home to tend to matters there; running errands; getting to bed; or spending some time with their husbands. So let them out *on time!*

Five Common Problems

In any group, you can anticipate certain problems. Here are some common ones that can arise, along with helpful solutions:

1. *The incomplete lesson*—Right from the start, establish the policy that if someone has not done the lesson, it is best for her not to answer the questions. But do try to include her responses to questions that ask for opinions or experiences. Everyone can share some thoughts in reply to a question like "Reflect on what you know about both athletic and spiritual training, and then share what you consider to be the essential elements of training oneself in godliness."

2. *The gossip*—The Bible clearly states that gossiping is wrong, so you don't want to allow it in your group. Set a high and strict standard by saying, "I am not comfortable with this conversation," or "We [not *you*] are gossiping, ladies. Let's move on."

3. *The talkative member*—Here are three scenarios and some possible solutions for each.

   a. The problem talker may be talking because she has done her homework and is excited about something she has to share. She may also know more about the subject than the others and, if you cut her off, the rest of the group may suffer.

   SOLUTION: Respond with a comment like: "Sarah, you are making very valuable contributions. Let's see if we can get some reactions from the others," or "I know Sarah can answer this. She's really done her homework. How about some of the rest of you?"

b. The talkative member may be talking because she has *not* done her homework and wants to contribute, but she has no boundaries.

SOLUTION: Establish at the first meeting that those who have not done the lesson do not contribute except on opinion or application questions. You may need to repeat this guideline at the beginning of each session.

c. The talkative member may want to be heard whether or not she has anything worthwhile to contribute.

SOLUTION: After subtle reminders, be more direct, saying, "Betty, I know you would like to share your ideas, but let's give others a chance. I'll call on you later."

4. *The quiet member*—Here are two scenarios and possible solutions.

a. The quiet member wants the floor but somehow can't get the chance to share.

SOLUTION: Clear the path for the quiet member by first watching for clues that she wants to speak (moving to the edge of her seat, looking as if she wants to speak, perhaps even starting to say something) and then saying, "Just a second. I think Chris wants to say something." Then, of course, make her a hero!

b. The quiet member simply doesn't want the floor.

SOLUTION: "Chris, what answer do you have on question 2?" or "Chris, what do you think about...?" Usually after a shy person has contributed a few times, she will become more confident and more ready to share. Your role is to provide an opportunity where there is *no* risk of a wrong answer. But occasionally a group member will tell you that she would rather not be called on. Honor her request, but from time to time ask her privately if she feels ready to contribute to the group discussions.

In fact, give all your group members the right to pass. During your first meeting, explain that any time a group member does not care to share an answer, she may simply say, "I pass." You'll want to repeat this policy at the beginning of every group session.

5. *The wrong answer*—Never tell a group member that she has given a wrong answer, but at the same time never let a wrong answer go by.

SOLUTION: Either ask if someone else has a different answer or ask additional questions that will cause the right answer to emerge. As the women get closer to the right answer, say, "We're getting warmer! Keep thinking! We're almost there!"

Learning from Experience

Immediately after each Bible study session, evaluate the group discussion time using this checklist. You may also want a member of your group (or an assistant or trainee or outside observer) to evaluate you periodically.

May God strengthen—and encourage!—you as you assist others in the discovery of His many wonderful truths.

Personal Notes

Personal Notes

Personal Notes

Personal Notes

_____

_____

_____

_____

_____

_____

_____

_____

_____

_____

_____

_____

_____

_____

_____

_____

_____

_____

_____

_____

_____

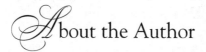

About the Author

Elizabeth George is a bestselling author and speaker whose passion is to teach the Bible in a way that changes women's lives. For information about Elizabeth's books or speaking ministry, to sign up for her mailings, or to share how God has used this book in your life, please write to Elizabeth at:

Jim and Elizabeth George Ministries
P.O. Box 2879
Belfair, WA 98528

Toll-free fax/phone: 1-800-542-4611
www.elizabethgeorge.com
www.jimgeorge.com

~

You can have an exciting prayer life!

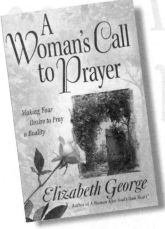

A Woman's Call to Prayer

Do you long for a meaningful prayer life but find that the demands of family, work, and home get in the way of your good intentions? Whether you're a prayer "wanna-be" who wonders how to take your first step into prayer or a seasoned prayer-warrior who aspires to continue in the battle, Elizabeth George will help you make your desire to pray a reality. You'll learn practical ways to—

- ✓ refresh your commitment to pray
- ✓ lift family and friends up to God
- ✓ discover God's will for your life
- ✓ worship God through prayer

Begin—or improve!—your journey of prayer. Elizabeth provides the inspiration, motivation, and step-by-step guidance you need to answer God's call to prayer.

A Woman's Call to Prayer
is available at your local Christian bookstore
or can be ordered from:

Jim and Elizabeth George Ministries
P.O. Box 2879
Belfair, WA 98528
Toll-free fax/phone: 1-800-542-4611
www.elizabethgeorge.com

Books by Elizabeth George

Beautiful in God's Eyes—The Treasures of the Proverbs 31 Woman
God's Wisdom for Every Woman's Life
Life Management for Busy Women
Loving God with All Your Mind
Powerful Promises™ for Every Woman
The Remarkable Women of the Bible
A Wife After God's Own Heart
A Woman After God's Own Heart®
A Woman After God's Own Heart® Deluxe Edition
A Woman After God's Own Heart® Prayer Journal
A Woman's Call to Prayer
A Woman's High Calling
A Woman's Walk with God
A Young Woman After God's Own Heart

Growth & Study Guides

God's Wisdom for Every Woman's Life Growth & Study Guide
Life Management for Busy Women Growth & Study Guide
Powerful Promises™ for Every Woman Growth & Study Guide
The Remarkable Women of the Bible Growth & Study Guide
A Wife After God's Own Heart Growth & Study Guide
A Woman After God's Own Heart® Growth & Study Guide
A Woman's Call to Prayer Growth & Study Guide
A Woman's High Calling Growth & Study Guide
A Woman's Walk with God Growth & Study Guide

A Woman After God's Own Heart® Bible Study Series

Walking in God's Promises—The Life of Sarah
Cultivating a Life of Character—Judges/Ruth
Becoming a Woman of Beauty & Strength—Esther
Discovering the Treasures of a Godly Woman—Proverbs 31
Nurturing a Heart of Humility—The Life of Mary
Experiencing God's Peace—Philippians
Pursuing Godliness—1 Timothy
Growing in Wisdom & Faith—James
Putting On a Gentle & Quiet Spirit—1 Peter

Books by Jim George

A Husband After God's Own Heart
A Man After God's Own Heart
God's Man of Influence

Books by Jim & Elizabeth George

Powerful Promises for Every Couple
Powerful Promises for Every Couple Growth & Study Guide
(Coming Spetember 2004)

Children's Books

God Loves His Precious Children
God's Wisdom for Little Boys
God's Wisdom for Little Girls (Elizabeth George)

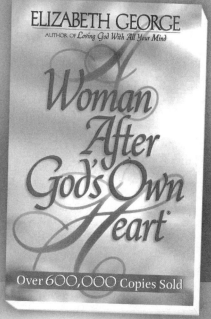

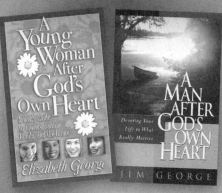
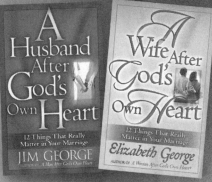

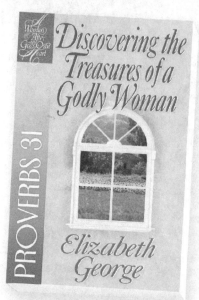